EXPLORING THE SOLAR SYSTEM

MERCURY

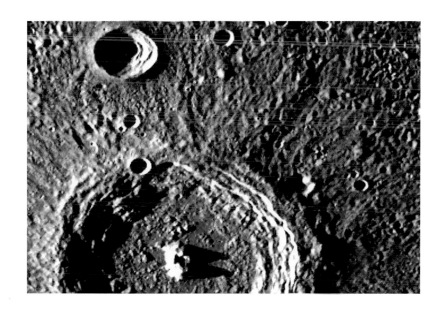

GILES SPARROW

Heinemann
LIBRARY

MERCURY

Published by Heinemann Library,
a division of Reed Educational & Professional Publishing,
Halley Court, Jordan Hill,
Oxford OX2 8EJ, UK
Visit our website at www.heinemann.co.uk/library

Produced by Brown Partworks
Project Editor: Ben Morgan
Deputy Editor: Sally McFall
Managing Editor: Anne O'Daly
Designer: Steve Wilson
Illustrator: Mark Walker
Picture Researcher: Helen Simm
Consultant: Peter Bond

© 2001 Brown Partworks Limited

Printed in Singapore

ISBN 0 431 12260 1 (hardback)   ISBN 0 431 12269 5 (paperback)
06 05 04 03 02 01   06 05 04 03 02 01
10 9 8 7 6 5 4 3 2 1   10 9 8 7 6 5 4 3 2 1

British Library Cataloguing in Publication Data

Sparrow, Giles
   Mercury. – (Exploring the solar system)
   1.Mercury (Planet) – Juvenile literature
   I.Title
   523.4'1

BELOW: *The planets of the Solar System, shown in order from the Sun:
Mercury, Venus, Earth, Mars, Jupiter, Saturn, Uranus, Neptune, Pluto.*

CONTENTS

*Some words are shown in bold, **like this.***
You can find out what they mean by looking in the glossary.

Where is Mercury?

Mercury is the closest planet to the Sun, **orbiting** many millions of kilometres closer than our own planet, Earth. It is the first of the four inner planets – the small, Earth-like worlds of the inner Solar System that are made mostly of rock. The other inner planets are Venus, Earth and Mars. Beyond Mars lies the **asteroid belt** – a gigantic circle of space rocks, or **asteroids**. Beyond this is the realm of the **gas giant** planets: Jupiter, Saturn, Uranus and Neptune. Further still is Pluto, the smallest and outermost planet. Mercury is the second smallest planet in the Solar System, after tiny Pluto.

Mercury does not follow a circular path as it orbits the Sun. Instead, its orbit is a stretched, oval shape called an **ellipse**. In fact, Mercury has the most stretched orbit of all the planets except Pluto. As a result, its distance from the Sun ranges from 46 million kilometres (29 million miles) to 70 million kilometres (43 million miles). The time a planet takes to complete one orbit of the Sun is the length of its year, and Mercury's year is almost exactly 88 days.

Getting to Mercury

The time it takes to reach Mercury depends on your method of transport, and on the positions of Earth and Mercury in their orbits when you set off.

Distance from Earth to Mercury
Closest   77 million km
             (48 million miles)
Furthest   222 million km
             (138 million miles)

By car at 113 km per hour (70 miles per hour)
Closest   **88 years**
Furthest   **253 years**

By rocket at 11 km per second (7 miles per second)
Closest   **79 days**
Furthest   **228 days**

Time for radio signals to reach Mercury (at the speed of light)
Closest   4 min. 18 sec.
Furthest   12 min. 22 sec.

Distance from the Sun

The diagram shows how far the planets are from the Sun. Mercury is the nearest of the four inner planets. The other inner planets are Venus, Earth and Mars.

Sun   Mercury   Venus   Earth   Mars   Jupiter   Saturn

0   1000 (621)   2000 (1243)

Distance in millions of kilometres (millions of miles)

The distance between Mercury and Earth varies even more and depends on the positions of both planets in their orbits. They are closest together when they line up on the same side of the Sun and furthest apart when they line up on opposite sides of the Sun.

Imagine you're going on a **mission** to Mercury. One of the problems you'll face will be catching up with the planet, because Mercury travels through space much faster than Earth. Earth moves around the Sun at around 30 kilometres (19 miles) per second, but Mercury races around at 48 kilometres (30 miles) per second. As well as needing a very powerful rocket, you will have to take a roundabout route. First your ship will fly past Venus, allowing its **gravity** to pull you forward and give you a burst of speed as you swing around the planet. You will have to plan your mission carefully and leave when Earth, Venus and Mercury are all in just the right positions.

*Mercury is the innermost of the Solar System's nine planets. This artist's impression also shows Venus, Earth, Earth's Moon, Mars and the **asteroid belt**.*

Size compared to Earth

Mercury's diameter:
4878 kilometres
(3030 miles)

Earth's diameter:
12,756 kilometres
(7926 miles)

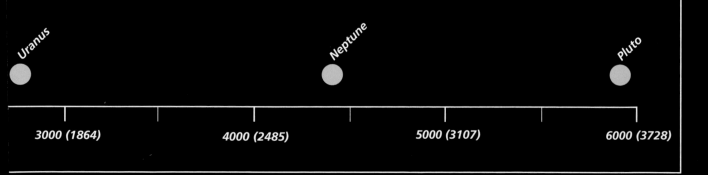

Uranus

Neptune

Pluto

3000 (1864)   4000 (2485)   5000 (3107)   6000 (3728)

First view

Before you start, you want to see what Mercury looks like from Earth. Although the planet is not too far, it's very difficult to spot, and many people go their whole lives without seeing it. The problem is that Mercury is always close to the Sun. The only chance of seeing it is to wait for the point in Mercury's **orbit** where it appears furthest from the Sun in our sky. At these times Mercury is visible as an orange star in the east just before sunrise, or in the west just after sunset. Mercury is actually quite bright, but dawn or dusk drowns out most of its light.

Very rarely, there's a chance to see Mercury pass in front of the Sun, an event known as **transit**. Never look directly at the Sun during a transit or at any other time – even with sunglasses. However, if you project the Sun's image onto white paper through a sheet of cardboard with a pinhole in it, you can safely see Mercury's silhouette during a transit.

ABOVE: *Mercury makes a rare appearance in this photograph of dawn breaking over the Australian outback.*

It's time to leave. A space shuttle takes you to your spacecraft, which has been built in orbit so that no fuel will be wasted escaping from Earth's **gravity**. Now that you're in space, Mercury is easy to see. All you have to do is cover the Sun with your hand, and Mercury appears as a bright 'star'. With a telescope you can see that Mercury is yellowish-grey, and it looks **crescent**-shaped because part of the planet is hidden by shadow. Like our Moon, Mercury goes through regular **phases** where different amounts of the planet's sunlit side are visible from Earth, depending on the positions of the two planets in their orbits.

*Your **mission** to Mercury begins on board a space shuttle, which will take you to your ship waiting in orbit.*

Getting closer

Your ship's rockets turn on, firing slowly and steadily to send you on a course to Venus. One of the strangest things about space travel is **zero gravity**. In zero gravity objects become weightless and float in mid-air, and there is no up or down. Although zero gravity can be fun, it sometimes makes astronauts feel sick, and months of zero gravity can cause your bones and muscles to weaken through lack of exercise. To keep you in shape your ship will spin around to create weak **artificial gravity**, but you need to exercise regularly as well.

The whole journey to Mercury will last several months. The detour to Venus will make the voyage longer than a straight trip to Mercury, but it is the only way to pick up enough speed to join Mercury in its orbit around the Sun, rather than just making a brief **flyby**. As your ship catches up with Venus and then swings around it towards Mercury, it actually borrows some of Venus's energy. This gives your speed an incredible boost, and it slows down Venus very slightly. There's no danger of getting trapped by Venus's gravity because you won't fly directly towards it.

With Venus behind you, you start to concentrate on Mercury. The phases, as well as faint blotches on the surface, are becoming visible to the naked eye. As you get closer the blotches gradually turn into craters. Now you can see that Mercury is covered in craters – in fact it looks like a twin of Earth's Moon.

*The craters on Mercury were made by **comets**, asteroids and **meteorites** that crashed into the planet*

A short blast from your **braking rockets** slows you down and puts you in **orbit** high above Mercury. Your ship's instruments indicate that Mercury's **gravity** is much stronger than you would expect for such a small planet. The strength of a planet's gravity depends on how much material, or **mass**, it contains. Mercury must have a lot of mass squeezed into it, making it one of the most **dense** planets in the Solar System.

You start to look at the surface in detail. Close up, the resemblance to the Moon is still strong – there are heavily cratered raised regions, called highlands, and open plains lying in between them. But as you look closer, you start to notice differences. Large cracks run across the landscape, often cutting through the middle of craters. Some are steep-sided valleys, while others are long, winding cliffs, raising one region of the planet's surface high above its surroundings.

Only one space probe has visited Mercury, and this was its first picture of the planet, taken from more than 5 million kilometres (3 million miles) away.

A range of mountains appears on the horizon. As your orbit carries you over them, the mountain range transforms into a huge ring that must be hundreds of kilometres wide. From high above it looks like a gigantic target.

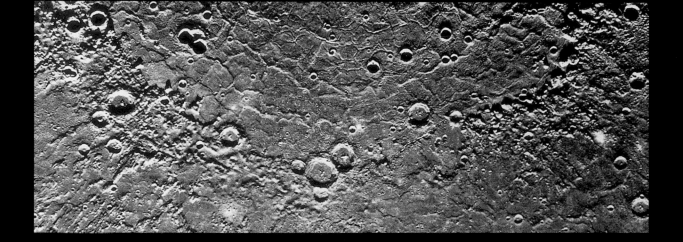

In the middle of this cosmic bullseye is a vast crater, 1340 kilometres (840 miles) across, with an open plain for its floor. This is the Caloris **Basin**, one of the largest **impact craters** in the Solar System.

ABOVE: *The mountain range that surrounds the Caloris Basin can be seen curving across this picture.*

You notice something odd. Although you are travelling around Mercury at high speed, the planet itself doesn't seem to be **rotating**. Mercury does rotate, but it turns very slowly, taking about 59 Earth days to make one complete turn. This sluggish rotation gives Mercury one of the longest days in the Solar System.

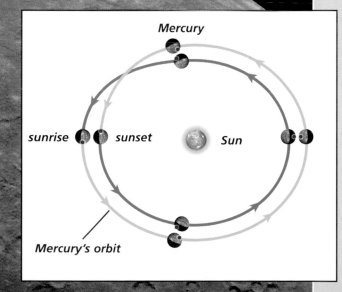

sunrise — sunset — Sun

Mercury

Mercury's orbit

Strange days

There are two ways of measuring daylength. You can measure how long a planet takes to rotate once – its **sidereal day** – or you can measure the time from one sunrise to the next. For most planets the two are about the same, but on Mercury they are very different. Imagine you're standing on Mercury at sunrise (left-most red spot in the diagram). You would have to wait a whole Mercurial year for sunset, and then another year before the next sunrise. In other words, a day on Mercury, from sunrise to sunrise, lasts twice as long as a Mercurial year!

Highlands and plains

It's time to go down to the surface. As you drop out of **orbit** towards the ground, you resist the temptation to head straight for the Caloris **Basin**, and instead land in one of the highland regions.

The dusty ground sinks slightly beneath your boots as you step outside, but it supports your weight. You have just over a third of your Earth weight on Mercury. You're more than twice as heavy as you would be on the Moon, but you can still bound around in huge jumps and strides.

Mercury has almost no air, so the sky is black and starry even at midday. There's no **atmosphere** to protect you from the Sun's deadly **radiation**, so a spacesuit is essential. The spacesuit also supplies you with breathable air and controls your body temperature. The Sun glows brilliantly in the sky – more than twice as large as it appears from Earth. The soil feels crunchy underfoot, and you stoop down to pick up a handful of it in your heavy glove. It seems to be a mix of powdered rocks of different sizes. This type of rock dust, called **regolith**, is also found on the Moon. It forms from the **debris** thrown out when **meteorites** and other objects from space smash into the ground. In some places you find large boulders known as **breccias**. These form when the regolith gets compressed into solid chunks by meteorite impacts.

ABOVE: *From your large spacecraft in orbit, you descend to Mercury's surface in a specially designed capsule called a lander.*

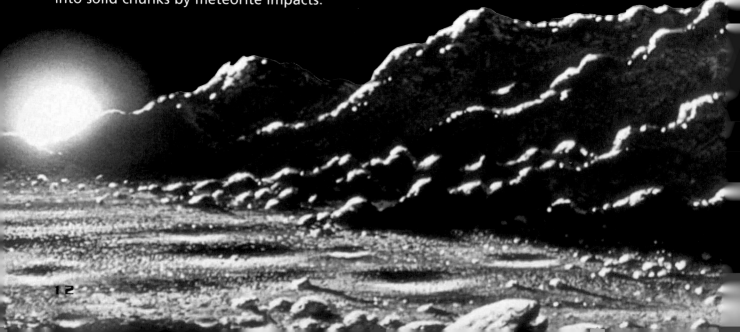

As you descended, you noticed that the gaps between the **impact craters** were not as smooth as they looked from a distance – they are peppered with craters made by meteorite impacts. These fall into two distinct types: large, ghostly rings that have been worn down or filled in by the regolith, and smaller, sharper craters that often cut across larger ones, showing they formed more recently.

You bound over to a small crater. It must be fairly recent – it's crisp and perfectly formed, with a bowl-shaped hole in the centre and a raised rim around it. Outside this is a circle of pale debris thrown out by the impact and some very small craters, often with oval or teardrop shapes. These are secondary craters, made by larger chunks of rock thrown out of the main crater during impact. Finally you trudge back to your lander to return to orbit.

The Sun is beginning to rise over the horizon in this artist's impression of Mercury's highlands.

Cliffhangers

After flying for a few minutes, you spot one of the steep cliffs that wind their way across Mercury's surface. It cuts across the middle of a crater, and you land nearby.

From the ground you get a better idea of the cliff's scale. It rises straight up from the floor of the crater for more than 305 metres (1000 feet). On Earth, cliffs like this often show different rock layers, or **strata**, but Mercury's cliffs show none. Strata appear in **sedimentary rock**, which forms from tiny **particles** of sand or mud that build up on the seafloor, layer by layer. On Mercury there are no oceans, so sedimentary rock cannot form.

You chip away at the cliff face with a pickaxe and take some samples back to your spacecraft to analyse. Your instruments reveal the different minerals that make up the rock, and the results are a surprise. Although the rock contains similar minerals to those in Earth rock, such as **silica**, one chemical is almost absent: iron.

*The winding area of raised ground running down through this picture is a **scarp**. Called Santa Maria Rupes, this scarp formed when a strip of Mercury's **crust** was pushed upward.*

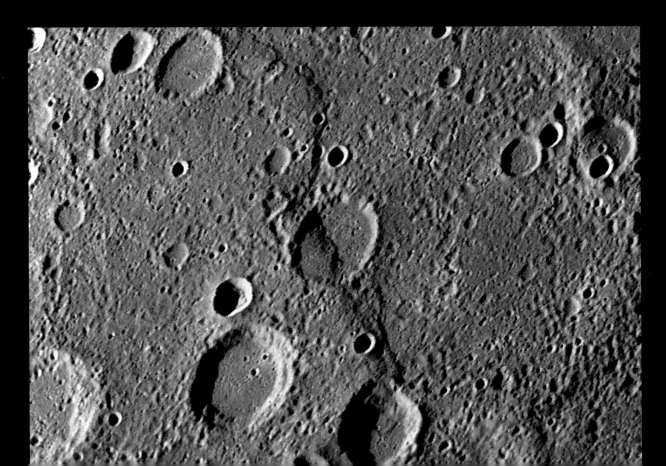

This cliff face in Norfolk, England, shows the distinct layers, or strata, that often appear in rock on Earth. Strata occur in rock that forms from layers of sediment building up on the seafloor. Mercury's cliffs have no strata.

Eugène Marie Antoniadi
(1870–1944)

The greatest observer of Mercury before the era of space exploration was probably Eugène Marie Antoniadi, a Greek-born French astronomer who made careful drawings of the planet between 1924 and 1929. Antoniadi is best known for revealing that the famous canals of Mars were just illusions. Antoniadi Ridge on Mercury (running down the right side of the picture below) is named after him.

The lack of iron is puzzling. It means that Mercury's surface rocks are very light, yet you discovered earlier that the planet as a whole is very **dense**. The only answer to the puzzle is that something very heavy must be hiding in Mercury's interior.

As you fly across the barren landscape again you notice more strange cracks in Mercury's surface. Long strips of the surface are raised up, with steep cliffs on either side. Many of these cliffs are even taller than the one you visited, towering several kilometres into the sky. Other areas seem to have slipped down below the surrounding terrain, forming steep-sided trenches. What force could have lifted up huge sections of Mercury's crust and caused others to collapse? Astronomers think the most likely explanation is that Mercury swelled up and then shrank early in its history.

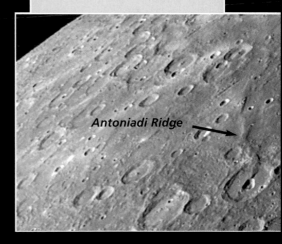

Antoniadi Ridge

Caloris Basin

It's time to look at Mercury's most impressive feature. The Caloris **Basin** is the second largest **impact crater** in the Solar System – only the Aitken Basin on the Moon's south **pole** is bigger. If an impact as big as the one that created the Caloris Basin happened on Earth, it could obliterate France and hurl **debris** right across the Atlantic Ocean.

The flat plain that fills the Caloris Basin is visible in the left of this picture, pockmarked with craters. Caloris Basin is about 1340 kilometres (840 miles) wide.

As you fly towards the basin you cross a new type of landscape. There are few craters here, but you see other features. Giant wrinkles run across the landscape, and in many places the ground appears buckled, thrown into a jumble of hills and hollows.

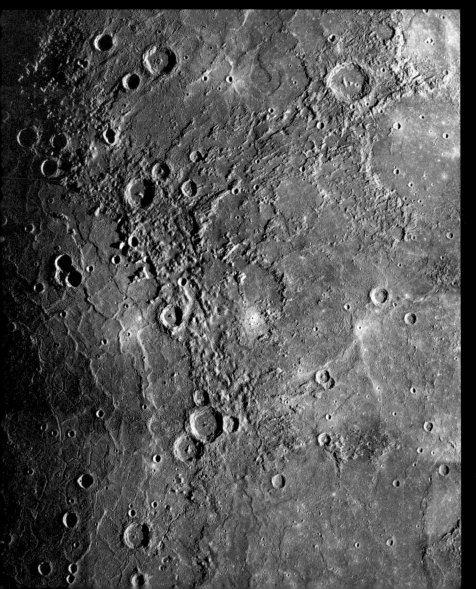

Past the jumbled hills is a smooth, flat area, broken by long chains of hills arranged around the basin likes spokes in a wheel. These hills, called the Van Eyck formation, were formed by material ejected from the huge impact that produced the Caloris Basin.

You reach the edge of the basin, which is marked by a range of mountains three kilometres (two miles) tall – about half the height of the Rockies in the USA. In a few places impact craters have gouged huge holes in the range. The mountain range is not very wide and you cross it quickly. Now you can see that the mountains form a vast circle about 1340 kilometres (840 miles) in **diameter**.

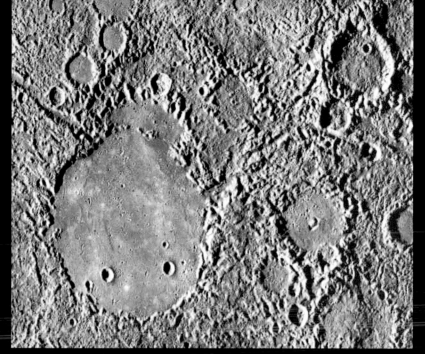

The interior of the basin is a surprise. You were expecting a vast, bowl-shaped hollow in the middle, but all you find is a flat plain of bare rock stretching in all directions. It is as though the whole crater has been filled in with cement.

Caloris is not the only major basin on Mercury. At least 15 others are known, and all have a flat plain in the middle. The plains probably formed from **lava** that filled in the basins after the impacts. The lava may have come from volcanoes triggered by the impacts, or perhaps the impacts were so violent that they melted large parts of Mercury's **crust**. The jumbled landscape of wrinkles and hills further out may have formed from semi-molten rock that didn't get hot enough to turn completely into lava.

Many of Mercury's largest craters, like the one above, have flat plains in the middle where they filled up with lava.

Weird Terrain

The Caloris Basin impact was so big that its effects were felt on the other side of the planet. Some shockwaves rippled all the way around Mercury's surface, while deeper shockwaves travelled straight through the planet's interior. Where the waves met up on the opposite side of Mercury they caused huge earthquakes. These earthquakes produced a jumbled, chaotic landscape that astronomers call the Weird Terrain (right).

What's inside Mercury?

The rock samples you collected on the surface indicate that Mercury has a lightweight outer layer, or **crust**. The cliffs, **regolith** and the rest of the crust are probably all made of the same minerals. But this means that Mercury's interior must be extra **dense** to account for the planet's high **mass**. There is only one possible explanation: the interior of Mercury must be a gigantic ball of metal.

Mercury is really a huge ball of metal surrounded by a thin coating of rock.

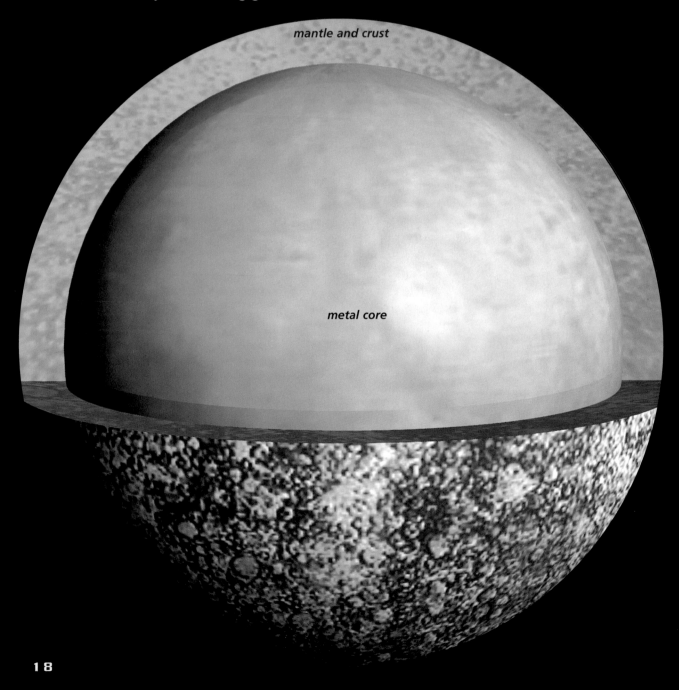

mantle and crust

metal core

Mercury's magnetism

Earth's strong **magnetic field** is caused by molten iron spinning around in the planet's core. Because Mercury spins so slowly, astronomers once thought it could not have a magnetic field. However, **space probes** discovered that Mercury does indeed have a magnetic field, though a very weak one. Astronomers think Mercury's weak magnetic field is frozen into the core, like the magnetic field in a bar magnet (right).

Astronomers think a huge iron **core** fills most of Mercury. There is little iron in Mercury's surface rocks, but iron is the only **element** heavy enough and common enough in the Solar System to make up Mercury's core. While the cores of other planets are relatively small, Mercury's must take up around three-quarters of the planet's width.

If you could split Mercury open and look inside you would see three different layers. In the middle is the core, which is mostly iron but also contains nickel and other elements. Some of these elements are **radioactive**, which causes them to release heat and keep the core warm. In larger planets this process releases so much heat that the core melts. However, Mercury loses heat into space quickly

Clues from craters

Craters can form in several ways. **Impact craters** are caused by collisions with **meteorites**, **asteroids** and **comets**, and volcanic craters form when volcanoes collapse into the hollow ground below them. All the craters on Mercury look like they were formed by impacts. You can estimate the ages of craters from the way they overlap: younger craters always lie on top of older ones, and they coat older craters with **debris**.

How impact craters form

Impact craters form when comets, meteorites or asteroids smash into planets and moons. Everything in space is travelling at tremendous speed, so when two objects hit each other, the collision is incredibly violent and releases huge amounts of energy. Asteroids, comets and meteorites usually vaporize and disappear completely during impact. The ground below gets squashed as it is hit, but then it springs back suddenly, throwing out masses of pulverized rock. This produces a bowl-shaped crater, and there is often a mountain in the middle where the ground bounced back. The walls of big craters are sometimes so steep that they crumble inwards, forming a pattern of steps called terraces.

ABOVE: *Comet Hale-Bopp crosses the night sky, seen from Earth in 1997. Mercury is especially prone to being hit by comets, which swoop close to the planet during their erratic **orbits** around the Sun.*

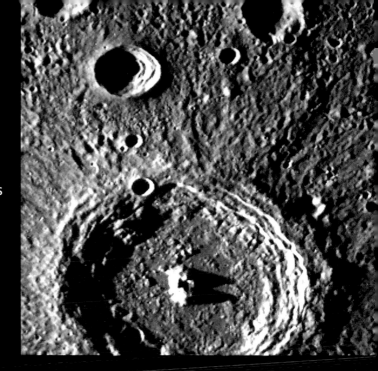

Mercury's highlands formed from a build-up of debris during a period of intense cratering called the **late heavy bombardment**. This happened around 4 billion years ago, when the young Solar System contained lots of asteroids and comets. The number of asteroids and comets gradually fell as they collided with planets, bringing the period of bombardment to an end. The thick layer of debris thrown into Mercury's highlands covered up a lot of old craters, but the largest ones still show through slightly, which explains the ghostly crater rings you saw earlier.

Towards the end of the late heavy bombardment there were just a few big asteroids left in the inner Solar System. When these collided with Mercury, they formed the planet's **basins**. The impacts obliterated thousands of ancient craters, and the basins filled with **lava**.

ABOVE: *This 98-km-wide (61-mile-wide) crater shows the crumbled terraced walls and central mountain typical of Mercury's large impact craters.*

Mercury's craters are different from those on Earth's Moon because the planet's higher **gravity** makes crater debris fall back closer to the impact site. There is also a difference in the objects that produce the craters. Because Mercury is further from the **asteroid belt**, it is less likely to be hit by asteroids. But it is much more likely to be hit by comets, which have stretched orbits that take them swooping close to the Sun and Mercury.

RIGHT: *The ghostly remains of ancient craters can be seen in the left of this picture.*

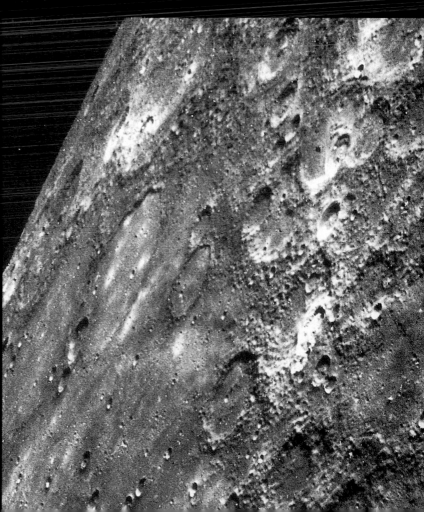

How Mercury formed

Like all the planets, Mercury formed from leftovers of the cloud of gas and dust that gave birth to the Sun.

About 4.5 billion years ago, the newly born Sun was left surrounded by a swirling disk of gas and dust. The disk's make-up varied, depending on the distance from the Sun. In the inner regions of this disk of space **debris**, the temperature was so hot that materials with a low boiling point turned into gases. These gases were then blown out of the inner Solar System by the **solar wind**, leaving solid materials behind.

This artist's impression shows a planetesimal orbiting the Sun in the young Solar System. Collisions with the debris around it have melted parts of the planetesimal's surface.

Over millions of years, the solid **particles** collided and stuck together, building up into large clumps of rock and metal called **planetesimals**. The planetesimals grew large enough to have their own **gravity**, and so pulled in more material, and sometimes they collided and stuck together. Eventually they became the planets of the inner Solar System, **orbiting** the Sun amid a cloud of smaller objects that rained down on them to form craters.

How scarps form

*The long winding cliffs that run across Mercury's surface are known as **scarps**. They formed early in the planet's history when Mercury swelled and shrank, causing its **crust** to split. Some sections of crust were forced upwards, producing long ridges with cliffs on both sides (top diagram). Other crust sections slipped downwards to form deep trenches bound by steep cliffs (bottom diagram).*

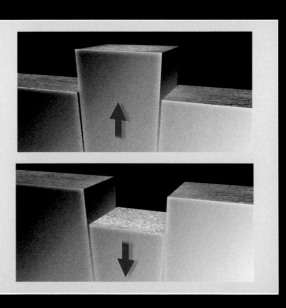

Something unusual must have happened to Mercury to give the planet its large metal core. One theory is that the material closest to the Sun had a higher proportion of metal. This is probably true, but then why does Venus, which also formed near the Sun, have a small metal core?

Another theory is that Mercury was once much larger, with a thicker **mantle** of rock. Perhaps a collision with another planet blasted most of Mercury's rock off into space, in the same way that a large chunk of Earth's mantle was probably blasted off by the collision that formed our Moon.

The Mariner 10 space probe took this picture of Mercury's south pole. The many craters bear witness to the planet's violent early history.

If Mercury did suffer some kind of violent catastrophe, it must have come early in the planet's history because it did not leave any traces on the planet's surface.

Mercury went through another very stressful period soon after it formed. Its interior seems to have heated up and expanded, possibly because it was being heated from outside by the **late heavy bombardment**. As Mercury swelled, its crust cracked apart and some parts sank down, creating steep-sided trenches. When Mercury eventually cooled down it shrank a little. This left the planet with more crust than it needed, and as it tried to shrink, large sections popped upwards like a cork out of a bottle. These formed raised strips of crust with cliffs on either side. These raised or sunken strips of land, known as scarps, explain the tall cliffs you saw earlier.

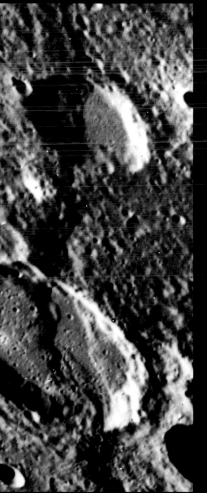

A scarp called Discovery Rupes runs through several craters in this photograph. Discovery Rupes formed when a section of crust was pushed up as the young Mercury cooled and shrank.

A day on Mercury

A Mercurial day lasts 176 Earth days. You don't have time to spend a whole Mercurial day on the surface, so you visit for a few Earth days instead. After landing and putting on your spacesuit, you step outside to watch the huge Sun rise slowly over the horizon.

Mercury's daytime temperature soars to 370°C (700°F) when the Sun comes up, but your spacesuit keeps you cool. The suit is heavy, but you hardly notice in the low **gravity**. You step into the shadow of a hill and stick a thermometer into soil that has not seen sunlight for two Mercurial years. With no blanket of air to keep the planet warm, Mercury's surface plummets to a freezing −180°C (−290°F) at night. From the shadow you see two brilliant 'stars' in the black sky, one white and one blue. The white one is Venus, and the blue one is your home − Earth.

ABOVE: From Mercury the Sun looks nearly three times wider than from Earth, yet the sky is black because Mercury is airless.

Planets spin around like tops as they **orbit** the Sun. Most of them spin at a tilt, and this is what causes seasons. Summer happens in the part of a planet that is tilted towards the Sun, and winter happens in the part that is tilted away. Mercury is almost exactly upright, so it has no seasons, and the Sun traces almost the same path across the sky every day of the year. You've landed on the **equator**, where the Sun rises from the horizon due east. Later in the long day the Sun will climb directly overhead before sinking slowly to a sunset due west.

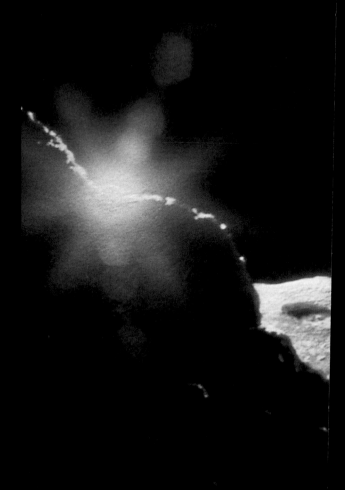

This artist's impression shows a sunrise on Mercury. Mercury is freezing cold at night, but when the sun rises it becomes one of the hottest planets in the Solar System.

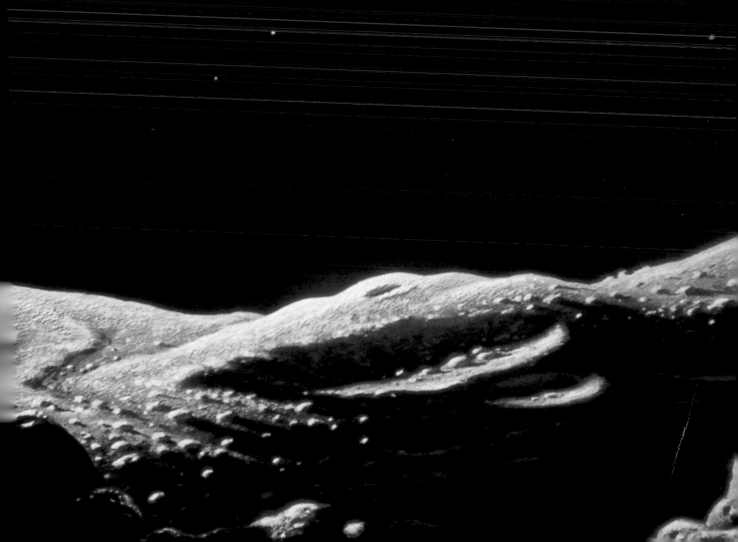

As you watch over a few Earth days you see that something very strange is happening. The Sun's climb up the sky slows down, and then it starts to sink back towards the horizon. A few days later it disappears completely, plunging the landscape back into darkness, but then it rises again!

This double sunrise is unique to Mercury. Because Mercury's orbit is an **ellipse**, the planet changes speed as it moves around the Sun. Mercury moves fastest when it is closest to the Sun – so fast, in fact, that its **rotation** cannot keep up. As Mercury races past, the Sun backtracks through the sky, before moving forwards again when the planet slows down.

Mercury's orbit

Like most planets, Mercury spins around like a top as it orbits the Sun, but it is almost exactly upright. In contrast, Earth is tilted over, which causes seasons – summer happens in the half of Earth that is tilted towards the Sun and winter happens in the half that is tilted away. Because Mercury has no tilt, it has no seasons.

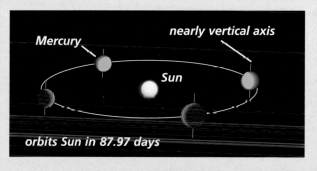

Mercury

nearly vertical axis

Sun

orbits Sun in 87.97 days

Atmosphere and climate

Because Mercury is the closest planet to the Sun, you might expect it to be the hottest planet in the Solar System. But it isn't. Although Mercury is scorching during the day, with an average midday temperature of about 370°C (700°F), the lack of a thick **atmosphere** keeps it from getting as hot as Venus. Venus's thick atmosphere also keeps its temperature high at night, but Mercury freezes as soon as the Sun sets.

Surprisingly, Mercury does actually have a sort of atmosphere – a sparse layer made of **atoms** of hydrogen, oxygen and sodium, mixed with a little potassium and helium. This shell of gas is emptier than the best **vacuums** created in Earth laboratories, so Mercury has no weather, and you can't see the atmosphere. Mercury's faint atmosphere is thought to form from atoms blasted off the planet's surface by the **solar wind**, a stream of electrified **particles** that continually flows out of the Sun.

This false-colour image of Mercury was produced by a special heat-sensitive telescope. The orange area is one of Mercury's hot spots, which receives more strong sunlight than the rest of the planet.

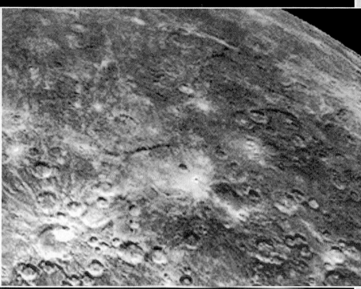

Changing colour

The solar wind has an interesting effect on Mercury: it gradually changes the planet's colour. As the surface rocks absorb solar wind particles, they change their chemical make-up and so change colour. The difference is small, but astronomers can exaggerate it by photographing Mercury with special cameras. In this image, green areas have been exposed to the solar wind for the longest, while red areas are relatively young.

You might think Mercury's very long nights would make its night side one of the coldest places in the Solar System, but you'd be wrong again. The dusty **regolith** traps a small amount of heat, keeping the surface of the planet warmer than it would otherwise be. The coldest places on Mercury are the north and south **poles**. Because the planet isn't tilted, the poles only ever see the Sun low on the horizon, and the bottoms of some craters are in permanent shadow. Some of these craters might shelter hidden deposits of ice, perhaps dropped on the planet by **comets** in the distant past.

Another strange feature of Mercury is that, as well as having cold north and south poles, it has hot spots on opposite sides of its **equator**. Because of the planet's

Myths, legends and early discoveries

Because Mercury is visible to the naked eye, it has been seen since ancient times. The Sumerians of Mesopotamia (now Iraq) knew of the planet as long as 5000 years ago, and ancient astronomers of India, China and many other lands also studied its movements.

Because Mercury appears only briefly at sunrise or sunset, it was often mistaken for two or more different objects. The Maya people of Central America saw the planet as four 'Skull Owls' – messengers from the underworld. Mercury's swift movement through the sky led to its being seen as a messenger. The Babylonians called it Nabu – the messenger god and the god of writing.

ABOVE: *The ancient Babylonians saw Mercury as the messenger god Nabu, shown here in a bronze carving.*

The Babylonians influenced Greek astronomy. When Mercury appeared in the evening sky the ancient Greeks called it Apollo, after the god of healing and prophecy. When it appeared in the morning they called it Hermes, after the messenger god. Mercury's modern name comes from the Roman equivalent of Hermes, but it has developed other meanings to do with swift movement. For example, the **element** mercury, once called quicksilver, is fast-moving and fluid, and someone with a mercurial temper is very changeable.

In the 1st century AD the Greek-Egyptian scientist Ptolemy suggested that the planets all circled Earth attached to transparent spheres made of crystal.

Ptolemy of Alexandria
(c.90–c.168)

The Greek-Egyptian scientist Ptolemy of Alexandria was perhaps the most influential astronomer of the ancient world. He summarized ancient knowledge of astronomy in his book Almagest. *Ptolemy put all the planets on spheres around the Earth, with small circles called epicycles to help explain their movements.*

Ptolemy thought Mercury lay just beyond the Moon, and he had to give it an incredibly complicated **orbit** to explain its movements. His model was improved by 4th-century astronomer Martianus Capella of Carthage (modern Tunisia), who suggested that Mercury and Venus circled the Sun while the Sun went around the Earth.

The invention of the telescope in the early 1600s transformed astronomy and revealed that Earth was in fact moving around the Sun. One of the clinching discoveries was that Venus shows changing **phases** like the Moon, but early telescopes were too weak to show the phases of Mercury. The little planet still had an important role to play, though. In 1627 the German astronomer Johannes Kepler predicted that Mercury would cross the Sun's face on 7 November 1631. Kepler died in 1630, but the **transit** he predicted was seen by the French astronomer and scientist Pierre Gassendi.

BELOW: *Hermes, shown in this fresco from a building in Italy, was the messenger god that the ancient Greeks associated with the planet Mercury.*

In 1639 an Italian priest named Ionnes Zupo became the first person to see the phases of Mercury. Astronomers continued to study the planet, but it was more than 100 years before anyone claimed to see markings on its surface.

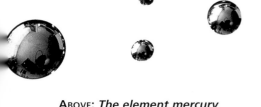

ABOVE: *The element mercury is a liquid metal at room temperature. It is named for its fast-moving, fluid nature.*

The search for Vulcan

Since Mercury is so difficult to see from Earth, can we be sure there isn't another planet even closer to the Sun that is permanently hidden by the Sun's blinding glare? For a while in the 19th century, many astronomers believed such a planet existed. Some claimed to have seen it, and it was even given a name – Vulcan, after the Roman god of fire.

The story of Vulcan began in 1859, when Doctor Lescarbault, a French amateur astronomer, saw a small round object passing across the face of the Sun while he was looking for **sunspots**. He reported his discovery to one of the most famous astronomers of the day, Urbain Leverrier.

ABOVE: Vulcan, the god of fire, is forging a helmet in this 18th-century engraving. He was also the god of metalworkers, because they used fire to shape the metal.

Leverrier was interested in the mathematics of **orbits**, and he was puzzled by Mercury. He knew that Mercury's perihelion – its closest point to the Sun – changes position slowly over thousands of years, but he couldn't figure out why. Leverrier thought that **gravity** from another planet might be responsible, and he calculated an orbit for Lescarbault's object. It was, he said, a planet smaller than Mercury, orbiting the Sun in only 19 days at a distance of about 21 million kilometres (13 million miles).

Urbain Leverrier (1811–1877)
The French astronomer Urbain Leverrier specialized in mathematics and rarely, if ever, looked through a telescope. He made his name in 1846 when he predicted the existence and position of Neptune from a careful analysis of distortions in the orbit of Uranus.

Although the **mass** of this single object was too small to disrupt Mercury's orbit all on its own, Leverrier thought that Vulcan might be the largest member of a swarm of **asteroids** orbiting close to the Sun.

A year later, in 1860, there was a total **eclipse** of the Sun in France. Eclipses give astronomers a rare opportunity to look for objects close to the Sun, but the astronomers who hoped to see Vulcan could not find it. The next reported sighting was not until 4 April 1875, when astronomers in Germany, Spain and England photographed a round dot crossing the face of the Sun. Amazingly, this **transit** was just a few hours later than one predicted by Leverrier and other supporters of Vulcan.

This artist's impression shows what some 19th-century astronomers believed was a new planet – Vulcan (top right).

Then American astronomers saw small round objects close to the Sun during a total eclipse in 1878, creating another flurry of interest. However, Leverrier had died the year before, and these new 'planets' did not match up with his theories. For a while there were no more sightings of Vulcan and people gradually lost interest. In 1916 Albert Einstein finally explained Mercury's curious orbit without needing a new planet. In his General Theory of Relativity, he stated that the distortion of Mercury's orbit was caused by the huge mass of the Sun bending space around it. Today, astronomers think the Vulcan sightings were a combination of sunspots, Near Earth Asteroids and **comets** close to the Sun.

Later observations

The first record of surface features on Mercury came from German astronomer Johann Schröter, who saw vague dark patches on the planet in the late 1700s. By the late 1800s many astronomers had reported markings on Mercury. Italian astronomer Giovanni Schiaparelli even claimed to see streaks criss-crossing the planet's surface. Although other astronomers disagreed, they all agreed on one thing – the marks, whatever they were, never changed, so they were always seeing the same face of Mercury.

BELOW: *At 305 metres (1000 feet) across, Arecibo is the largest telescope dish on Earth. The vast dish focuses radio waves onto a detector suspended overhead.*

Giovanni Schiaparelli
(1835–1910)

The Italian astronomer Giovanni Schiaparelli is best known for his observation of so-called canals on Mars. He thought he saw straight lines on the surface of the planet and named them canali, the Italian word for channels. This was mistranslated as canals, and so sparked a wave of interest in the possibility of intelligent life on Mars. Schiaparelli sketched similar markings on the surfaces of Mercury and Venus, but they all turned out to be illusions.

Some astronomers suggested Mercury must therefore **rotate** at the same speed as Earth, but Schiaparelli had a better theory. He thought Mercury had one face locked towards the Sun. According to this theory, Mercury would rotate once each time it **orbited** the Sun, so its **sidereal day** and its year would be equal. It also meant Mercury would have an icy cold dark side that never saw sunlight.

Schiaparelli's theory was accepted until 1962, when astronomers found that Mercury's 'dark side' was warmer than expected. In 1965 the world's biggest telescope dish – the Arecibo telescope in Puerto Rico – was used to study Mercury. Arecibo was used to beam radio waves at Mercury and monitor the echoes, a technique known as **radar** astronomy. Changes in the echoes allowed astronomers to work out that the planet's rotation period is actually 59 Earth days – two thirds of a Mercurial year.

Although one **space probe** (*Mariner 10*) visited Mercury in the 1970s, telescopes remain the best way of studying the planet. Radio telescopes have been used to measure the temperature of the unphotographed half of Mercury, revealing that it is probably covered with a blanket of powdery **regolith**, and radar astronomy has been used to map the height and roughness of Mercury's surface. The most exciting recent discovery is that Mercury has bright patches at its **poles** that match up with the positions of deep craters. The floors of these craters probably never see sunlight and may harbour ice deposited by **comets**.

Probes to Mercury

magnetic sensor

solar panel

The Mariner 10 *space probe came within 327 kilometres (203 miles) of Mercury and was able to take amazing close-up pictures of its surface features.*

radio antenna

TV camera

So far only one **space probe** has visited Mercury – *Mariner 10*. This may seem surprising, given that Mercury is one of our closest neighbours in space. However, as you saw earlier, getting up enough speed to reach the planet is quite a challenge. In fact, *Mariner 10* did not even try to catch up with Mercury. Instead it **orbited** the Sun in the opposite direction to Mercury, which sent it flying past the planet three times in twelve months.

The launch of *Mariner 10* took place on 3 November 1973. The probe took advantage of an unusual alignment between Earth, Venus and Mercury in early 1974. First it flew to Venus, where it used Venus's **gravity** to slow itself down and redirect it toward Mercury's orbit. This is the same principle, known as a **gravity assist**, that was later used to send probes to the outer planets, but in this case the technique was used to slow down the probe rather than speed it up.

Despite several problems during the flight, the probe passed Venus on 5 February 1974 and approached Mercury for the first time in late March. One of the first surface details the probe spotted was a bright **impact crater** named Kuiper. *Mariner 10* went on to photograph 40 per cent of the planet's surface, and discovered Mercury's **magnetic field** and thin **atmosphere**.

Six months after the first **flyby** of Mercury, the probe and planet whizzed past each other again. This time *Mariner 10* photographed the south **pole** of Mercury.

Gerard Kuiper (1905–1973)

*Dutch-born American scientist Gerard Kuiper was a member of the Mariner 10 ground control team. Sadly, he died just six weeks after the probe was launched. Kuiper was a pioneering planetary astronomer who discovered new moons orbiting Uranus and Neptune and atmospheres around Mars and Titan (one of Saturn's moons). As an adviser to NASA, he correctly predicted that Mercury would show evidence of impact craters and **lava** flows.*

Because of its unusual orbit and **rotation**, the same parts of Mercury were sunlit during each flyby, so half of the planet has never been seen.

Six months later *Mariner 10* flew past Mercury for the last time, passing close to the night side, and returned more information about the planet's magnetic field and atmosphere. Then the probe's fuel ran out, which sent it into a spinning orbit around the Sun, where it remains to this day.

This artist's impression shows the Mariner 10 probe during one of its encounters with Mercury.

Could humans live there?

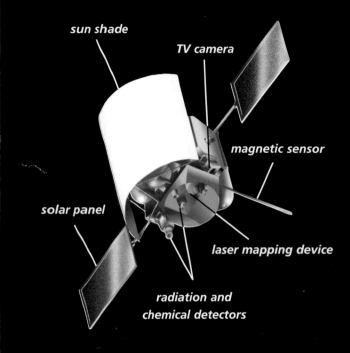

sun shade

TV camera

magnetic sensor

solar panel

laser mapping device

radiation and
chemical detectors

ABOVE: *An artist's impression of the design for the MESSENGER probe shows some of its main features.*

Mercury would be a dangerous and difficult world to colonize, but a human landing there would not be impossible. Confirmation of ice at the planet's **poles** would make the idea of a crewed **mission** to Mercury much more feasible. Ice not only could provide water, but also could be broken down to produce oxygen for breathing and rocket fuel for the return journey. A landing at one of the poles would also make conditions easier for the explorers, because the poles do not get as scorchingly hot as the **equator**.

A human mission to Mercury is unlikely in the near future because there is still a lot that can be learned about the planet by sending **space probes**. A new probe mission to Mercury, called *MESSENGER* (from an abbreviation of Mercury Surface, Space Environment, Geochemistry, and Ranging), is planned for launch in 2004.

MESSENGER will use five **gravity assists** – two from Venus, one from Earth and two from Mercury itself – to increase its speed to a point where it can catch up with and go into **orbit** around Mercury. It will then spend at least a year collecting data, using instruments that can detect chemicals and **radiation** in Mercury's **atmosphere** and on its surface, and using a **laser** mapping device to study the shape of the planet's surface. *MESSENGER* should fill in many of the gaps in our current knowledge of Mercury.

The cratered surface of Mercury is lit by its close neighbour, the Sun, in this artist's impression.

Glossary

artificial gravity force generated by a spaceship so that astronauts can stand on the floor instead of floating in midair

asteroid large chunk of rock left over from when the planets formed

asteroid belt ring of asteroids that orbit the Sun between the orbits of Mars and Jupiter

astrologer someone who practises an ancient tradition that people and events are influenced by the positions of planets, moons and stars

atmosphere layer of gas trapped by gravity around the surface of a planet

atom tiny particle of matter

basin large impact crater that filled up with lava

braking rockets rockets used to slow a spaceship down by firing forwards

breccia type of rock that forms when rock dust and stones are fused together by the heat and pressure of a meteorite impact

comet large chunk of ice left over from when the planets formed. Comets grow long, glowing tails when near the Sun.

crescent curved shape like one segment of an orange

crust solid outer surface of a planet or moon

debris fragments of rock, dust, ice, or other materials

dense having a lot of weight squeezed into a small space

diameter length of an object measured by drawing a straight line through its centre

eclipse effect caused by a planet or moon moving in front of the Sun and casting a shadow on another object

element chemical that cannot be split into other chemicals

ellipse stretched circle or oval

equator imaginary line around the centre of a planet, moon or star midway between the poles

flyby mission in which a space probe passes close to a planet but is travelling too fast to get caught by gravity and go into orbit

gas giant huge planet made out of gas. Jupiter and Saturn are gas giants.

gravity force that pulls objects together. The heavier or closer an object is, the stronger its gravity, or pull.

gravity assist flyby in which a spacecraft uses a planet's gravity to pick up speed

impact crater crater made when a comet, asteroid or meteorite smashes into a planet or moon

laser narrow, concentrated beam of light of a particular wavelength (colour)

late heavy bombardment period in the Solar System's early history in which the planets were bombarded by comets and asteroids

lava molten rock that pours onto a planet's surface

magnetic field region around a planet, moon or star where a compass can detect the north pole

mantle part of a planet or moon located between the core and the crust

mass measure of the amount of matter in an object. The mass of an object can be measured as weight when the object is on a planet.

meteorite space rock that lands on the surface of a planet or moon

mission expedition to visit a specific target in space, such as a planet, moon, star or comet

orbit path an object takes around another when it is trapped by the heavier object's gravity; or, to take such a path

particle tiny fragment of an atom. Particle can also mean a speck of dust or dirt.

phase the amount of the sunlit side of a planet or moon that an observer can see

planetesimal small, planet-like ball of debris that formed in the early Solar System

pole point on the surface of a planet, moon or star that coincides with the top or bottom end of its axis

radar technology using short pulses of radio waves to work out an object's position or shape

radiation energy released in rays from a source. Heat and light are types of radiation.

radioactive chemical unstable chemical that emits dangerous types of radiation

regolith top layer of fragmented rocky soil formed from meteorite impacts

rotation movement of a planet, moon or star turning around its centre, or axis

scarp line of cliffs

sedimentary rock type of rock formed from build-up of sediment on the seafloor

shockwave powerful pulse of energy that spreads out from an explosion, collision or other source

sidereal day time taken for a planet to make one complete rotation

silica common mineral found in rock on Earth and other planets. Sand is made of silica.

solar wind constant stream of particles that travel out of the Sun and through the Solar System at very high speed

space probe robotic vehicle sent from Earth to study the Solar System

strata distinct layers in sedimentary rock

sunspot dark spot on the Sun's surface where the temperature is slightly lower

transit movement of a planet directly in front of the Sun, as seen from Earth

vacuum region containing almost no matter. Space is a vacuum.

zero gravity absence of the effects of gravity, resulting in weightlessness

Books and websites

Couper, Heather, and Henbest, Nigel. *The DK Space Encyclopedia.* London: Dorling Kindersley, 1999.
Englebert, Phyllis. *The Handy Space Answer Book.* London: The Gale Group, 1997.
Furniss, Tim. *The Solar System – Spinning Through Space.* London: Hodder Wayland (Hodder & Stoughton Children's Division), 1999.
Kerrod, Robin. *Our Solar System – Near Planets.* London: Belitha Press Ltd, 2000.
nssdc.gsfc.nasa.gov/photo_gallery/ – NASA NSSDC Photo Gallery
sd-www.jhuapl.edu/MESSENGER/ – *MESSENGER*
seds.lpl.arizona.edu/nineplanets/nineplanets/mercury.html – Nine Planets (Mercury)
www.kidport.com/RefLib/Science/Space/Mercury.htm – The Planet Library, Mercury
www.windows.ucar.edu/ - Windows to the Universe

Index

Picture Credits
Key: t – top, b – below, c – centre, l – left, r – right. **NASA**: 4–5b, 7, 12, 36t, JPL/California Institute of Technology 2, 34, JPL/Northwestern University 1, 14, 15b, 16, 17t, 17b, 21t, 23t, 23b, 27, Mark Robinson/Northwestern University 3, 9, 10–11; **SOHO***: 4l; **Corbis**: Araldo de Luca 29br, Michael Freeman 28t; **Mary Evans Picture Library**: 30t; **Science Photo Library**: 8b, 28b, 30h, 31, 33, 35t, Dr Jeremy Burgess 29t, Vaughan Fleming 29bl, John Foster 24t, Mark Garlick 20b, 22t, David A. Hardy 12-13, 24–25, 36b, Bruce Iverson 19, M. Ledlow et al NRAO 26–27, NASA 11t, 21b, 35b, John Sanford 20t, Dr Seth Shostak 32–33, Robin Scagell 8t, Simon Terrey 15t. Front Cover: NASA, Mark Robinson/Northwstern University. Back Cover: NASA, JPL/California Institute of Technology. *SOHO is a project of international cooperation between ESA & NASA.